S0-ATD-548

Earth Mirth
The Ecology Riddle Book

by Mike Thaler
America's Riddle King

illustrated by Rick Brown

A TRUMPET CLUB SPECIAL EDITION

This book is dedicated to
Mother Nature and all her children.

No part of this publication may be reproduced in whole or in part, or stored in a retrieval system, or transmitted in any form or by any means, electronic, mechanical, photocopying, recording, or otherwise, without written permission of the publisher. For information regarding permission, write to W.H. Freeman and Company, 41 Madison Avenue, New York, NY 10010.

ISBN 0-590-33903-6

Text copyright © 1994 by Mike Thaler.
Illustrations copyright © 1994 by Rick Brown.
All rights reserved. Published by Scholastic Inc., 555 Broadway, New York, NY 10012, by arrangement with Scientific American Books for Young Readers, an imprint of W.H. Freeman and Company.

TRUMPET and the TRUMPET logo are registered trademarks of Scholastic Inc.

12 11 10 9 8 7 6 5 4 3 2 1   7 8 9/9 0 1 2/0

Printed in the U.S.A.   40

First Scholastic printing, April 1997

When is the Earth sad?

When it's down in the dumps.

When does the air get tired?

When it's exhausted.

What do you call it when the air is filled with rabbits?

Hare pollution.

What do you call it when the air is filled with pigs?

Swa-hog.

How does a magician get his car to run with less pollution?

He performs an elec-trick.

When is a boat cheapest to run?

When it's on sail.

What do you call a sun-powered tooth?

A solar molar.

What one habit does every creature on Earth share?

Our habit-at.

What do you call people who waste water?

Drips.

What do you call a bunch of bikers who celebrate Earth Day?

A recycle gang.

What do you call a large creature that recycles glass?

A hippo-bottle-mus.

What French dance recycles aluminum?

The can-can.

What do you call a one-eyed monster that recycles newspapers?

A recyclops.

Knock, knock.
Who's there?
Trash can.
Trash can who?

Trash can ruin the world.

What do polluting parrots and pigs pack things in?

Polly-sty-rene.

What kind of fishin' can kill all the fish?

Nuclear fishin'.

What kind of actor can kill the audience?

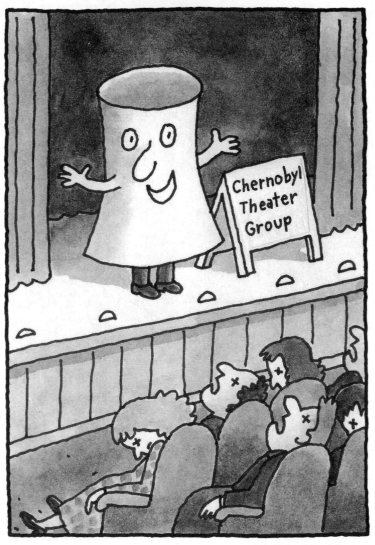

A nuclear re-actor.

What nation will allow the destruction of our environment?

Procrast-nation.

What nation can change the world?

Your imagi-nation.

How can you get into the swim of energy saving?

By joining a car pool.

What do you call it when the world is peaceful and happy?

Earth mirth.

What race is everyone in?

The human race.

What connects every living thing?

The food chain.

What do you call someone who eats automobiles?

What do you call someone who eats aluminum?

A can-nibble.

If the Earth took karate, what's the best it could be?

What subject did Professor Mouse teach?

Eek-ology.

Knock, knock. Who's there?
Garden. Garden who?

Garden the environment is important.

Where do you mail organic garbage?

At the compost office.

What station is the last stop for trees?

De-forest-station.

What is defoliation?

When the leaves leave.

Why do trees sleep in groups?

For-rest.

What rain forest do pigs help protect?

The Hamazon.

What is it?

1

2

3

1. A radioactive cloud.   2. Saving the spotted towel.   3. The food chain.

4. Radioactive dating.   5. A cover crop.   6. Decomposer.

What three letters run everything?

What two letters help nature's recyclers?

What kind of people are against alternative energy?

Fossil fools.

What do you call an oil truck that leaks all over town?

A city slicker.

What is recycling?

A pollution solution.

Why was Dr. Frankenstein an environmentalist?

Because he made his monster from recycled parts.

In *The Wizard of Oz,* what would Dorothy's friends worry about today?

The tin man would worry about filling up a landfill. The lion would be worried about becoming extinct. And the scarecrow would be worried about pesticides.

Who was the messiest super hero?

Trash Gordon.

What's the home of country garbage?

Trashville.

Why did the mother cat get a ticket?

For littering.

What do you call people's concerns for the ozone layer?

Atmos-fears.

Knock, knock.
Who's there?
Aerosol.
Aerosol who?

When you spray dangerous chemicals, the aerosol messed up.

What do you call a polluting car for hire?

A toxic cab.

What king causes bad air?

Smo-king.

What does a cigar smoker put into the air?

Cigar-bags.

What subject did the oil tanker fail in school?

Spilling.

How does the Earth get undressed?

By strip mining.

What do you call a person that steals Earth, air, and water?

A pol-looter.

What kind of ants can ruin the world?

Pollute-ants.

What sea are we all sailing in?

The galax-sea.

What tree grows in your imagination?

Poet-tree.

What do you call the poetry of the galaxies?

Uni-verse.

What can you hope to find in the Earth's checkbook?

The balance of nature.

How can the Earth get in shape?

By reducing its waist.

What ability does everyone on Earth have to help the environment?

Response-ability.

What should every home be?

A conservation station.

How does nature talk to you?

Through an echo-system.

What kind of vehicle can we all ride to a better life?

A recycle.